# THE ASHE BROTHERS

## How Arthur and Johnnie Changed Tennis Forever

by Judy Allen Dodson
illustrated by David Wilkerson

CAPSTONE EDITIONS
a capstone imprint

**BAM!** The ball sailed over the net.

Fans jumped to their feet and gave a standing ovation. Arthur Ashe had done it! He had made history! On September 8, 1968, he became the first Black man to win a Grand Slam title at the US Open.

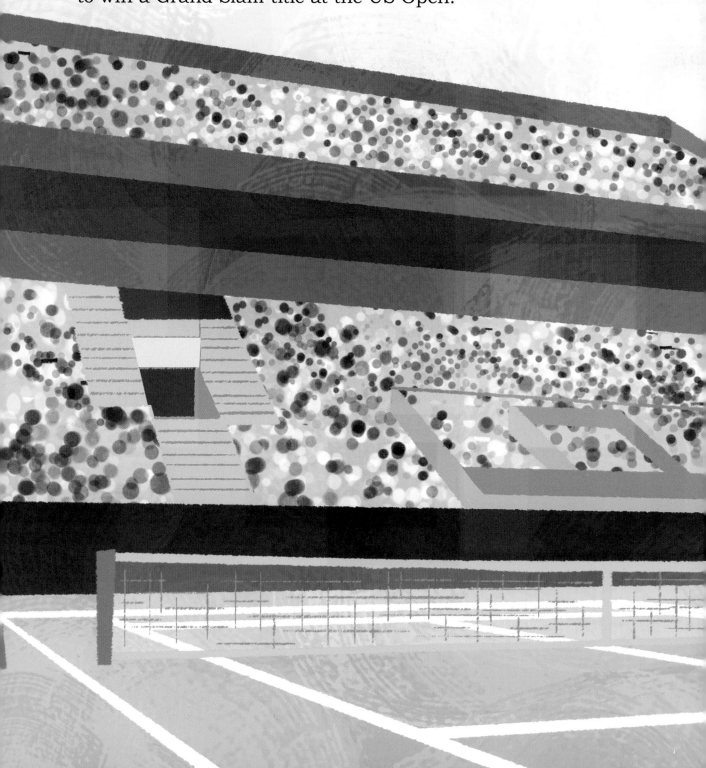

But Arthur's journey to the top of the tennis world wasn't an easy one, and his younger brother, Johnnie, was there every step of the way.

Twenty-five years earlier, when Arthur was born, the United States was segregated. Jim Crow laws kept Black and white people separate.

Arthur and Johnnie grew up surrounded by *COLORED ONLY* and *WHITE ONLY* signs—on water fountains, restrooms, and tennis courts.

**WHITE ONLY**

And in 1950, when Arthur was
six and Johnnie only one, their
mother, Mattie, died. In his
sadness, Arthur turned quiet
and shy. But when he stood
on the court with a racket
and a tennis ball in his
hand, he felt at home.

But tennis was mostly whites ONLY.

Except in Brook Field Park, the largest segregated playground in all of Richmond, Virginia, where Arthur and Johnnie just happened to live.

As the Brook Field Park police officer, their father, Arthur Ashe Sr., protected the park and the kids in it, including his sons. For their safety—on the court and off—he stressed:

No loud outbursts.
No cheating.
No shows of anger.
Do the right things for the right reasons.

As he grew, Arthur became very good at tennis. He zipped around the court, laser-focused, ready for each shot coming his way. When he threw the ball high in the air—**WHAM!** It zoomed like a rocket over the net.

But Johnnie was a rocket launcher too. He became Arthur's built-in tennis partner and biggest fan. And when Johnnie served the ball—**WHACK!** It shot through the air like lightning.

And no matter the outcome, Arthur and Johnnie walked off the court the same way they entered—as brothers and best friends.

By the time he was thirteen, Arthur had played and beaten everyone in his neighborhood. Johnnie wasn't always free to play tennis, and Arthur knew he needed new opponents and new challenges.

He searched for a good game of tennis at nearby Grant Park. But the segregation at the time made it almost impossible.

"You can't play here. You have to be white to play here. You better go back to Brook Field before you get into trouble," the Grant Park official said.

Arthur didn't argue. But for the first time, he felt what being born Black meant.

Johnnie wouldn't let Arthur quit. He knew his brother was special.

So special that by age fifteen, Arthur was ranked the fifth best player in the United States in his age group.

Just two years earlier, in 1956, Althea Gibson had become the first Black woman to win a Grand Slam title. But no Black man had defeated the all-white men's tennis establishment.

Arthur's father, neighbors, and coaches were convinced Arthur could do it. He could be the one to break the color barrier in men's tennis.

That filled Johnnie with pride. He thought Arthur could do it too.

With his brother's support, Arthur reluctantly made a decision that would keep them apart for a year—and then much longer, although they didn't know it at the time.

In the fall of 1960, Arthur left for a year of training in St. Louis, Missouri. There he could play tennis year-round on indoor courts. He could also compete against top players, unlike in segregated Richmond.

In 1961, Arthur made another move. He enrolled in the University of California, Los Angeles (UCLA). To help pay for college, he also enrolled as a Reserve Officers' Training Corp (ROTC) cadet.

He continued inching closer to his goal.

In 1963, Arthur became the first Black player ever selected to play on the U.S. Davis Cup team, the premier international team event in men's tennis.

By 1965, he was the number-two player in the country. That same year, he . . .

. . . won both the National Collegiate Athletic Association (NCAA) singles and doubles titles.

. . . and helped UCLA win the team NCAA tennis championship.

Back in Virginia, Johnnie cheered the loudest, just like when they were younger.

But the world was changing. The U.S. was in the middle of the Civil Rights Movement and the Vietnam War.

Like Arthur, Johnnie wanted to make a difference. At seventeen, he enlisted in the Marines. The following year, he deployed to Southeast Asia to fight on the front lines.

With bullets whizzing past his head, Johnnie proved he too was a champion—a survivor.

Despite the distance between them, the brothers were as close as ever. They wrote long letters to each other and talked on the phone as often as they could. Arthur prayed for Johnnie's safe return.

But then everything Arthur had worked so hard for almost
slipped right out of his grasp . . .

In the spring of 1967, Arthur had fifteen months left as an Army lieutenant. But he had never been called to war. Johnnie was already on active duty, and the military didn't like to send brothers into combat zones at the same time.

But Johnnie's tour was ending.

If Arthur were called to fight, he might never play tennis again. He might never win a Grand Slam major championship and break the color barrier.

Johnnie couldn't let that happen.

So, without telling his brother why, Johnnie signed up for a second tour of duty in Vietnam. Arthur wouldn't have to fight in the war—his brother would do it for him. Arthur was free to focus on tennis.

And focus he did.

On September 8, 1968, on a sunny day at the West Side Tennis Club in New York, Arthur took to the court. Fans watched as he served twenty-six aces, lobbed overhead shots, volleyed at the net, and created angles with his topspin forehand.

It was a grueling five-set match, and then . . .

Game!

Set!

Match!

The crowd leapt
to its feet.

Watching the match from his barracks at Camp Lejeune in North Carolina, Johnnie leapt to his feet too. His big brother had done it! Arthur had become the first Black man to win a Grand Slam title, smashing the color barrier in men's tennis.

Together, the Ashe brothers made history and changed the game of tennis forever.

As boys at Brook Field Park, when Arthur threw the ball high in the air, **WHACK!** It zoomed like a rocket over the net. And Johnnie fired it right back.

As men with many miles between them, when life served Arthur an impossible drop shot, **BAM!** Johnnie was still right there—as his brother's built-in partner and biggest fan.

# TIMELINE

**1943**—Arthur Robert Ashe Jr. is born in Richmond, Virginia, to parents Arthur Ashe Sr. and Mattie Cordell Cunningham Ashe.

**1948**—Johnnie Ashe is born.

**1950**—Mattie Ashe dies. Arthur meets his first tennis coach, Ron Charity.

**1953**—Arthur is invited to tennis summer camp at the home of Dr. Robert Walter Johnson, former coach to tennis champion Althea Gibson.

**1958**—Arthur becomes the first Black player at the Maryland boys' championships, his first integrated tennis competition.

**1961**—Arthur is named to the Junior Davis Cup team. He attends UCLA and joins the tennis team, becoming the number-three singles player.

**1963**—Arthur becomes the first Black player ever selected for the U.S. Davis Cup team.

**1965**—Johnnie enlists in the Marines. He is sent overseas to serve during the Vietnam War.

**1967**—Johnnie reenlists in the Marines, signing up for a second tour of duty in Vietnam.

**1968**—Arthur wins a Grand Slam title, becoming the first Black man to win the US Open. Johnnie returns from Vietnam and is stationed at Camp Lejeune, North Carolina.

**1969**—Arthur turns pro and is discharged from the Army. He cofounds the National Junior Tennis League (NJTL).

**1970**—Arthur becomes the first Black man to win the Australian Open.

**1975**—Arthur becomes the first Black man to win Wimbledon, the oldest and most prestigious tennis tournament in the world.

**1980**—Arthur retires from tennis. Johnnie continues his Marine Corps career and becomes a company commander.

**1985**—Arthur is inducted into the International Tennis Hall Of Fame. After serving for twenty years, Johnnie retires from Marines as Captain.

**1992**—Arthur is named Sportsman of the Year by *Sports Illustrated*.

**1993**—Arthur dies in New York at 49 years old.

**1996**—A 12-foot-tall bronze sculpture of Arthur Ashe is installed along along Monument Avenue in his home city of Richmond, Virginia.

**1997**—Arthur Ashe Stadium, a 23,771-seat tennis arena opens at Flushing Meadows–Corona Park in Queens, New York, and serves as the main arena for the US Open.

**2019**—Arthur Ashe Boulevard, a historic street in Richmond, Virginia, is approved by the Richmond City Council.

# A NOTE FROM THE AUTHOR

**"Start where you are. Use what you have. Do what you can."—Arthur Ashe**

As a child, my love of tennis began with watching old clips of Arthur Ashe. (In fact, as a child himself, Arthur played at the Algonquin Tennis Club in Durham, North Carolina—near where I currently live.) I loved his style of play, his speed to the ball, his gentle touch at the net, and the precision of each well-placed shot. I idolized him for many reasons, the most important being that he was Black like me. In tennis and on TV, that was rare.

It wasn't until many years later that I discovered through ESPN's *30 for 30* series that Arthur had a younger brother named Johnnie. I will never forget the pride I saw on Johnnie's face when he talked about Arthur and their father. Arthur Ashe Sr. raised his boys to "do the right things for the right reasons." That's exactly what Johnnie did. By signing up for a second tour in Vietnam, he allowed Arthur the freedom to focus on his own dream—becoming the first Black man to break the color barrier in tennis.

I wanted children to know the Ashe brothers' remarkable story. I needed to shine a bright light on the unconditional love Johnnie had—and still has—for his brother. Johnnie's sacrifice, which few people, including Arthur, knew about, changed the course of history. It helped make it possible for Arthur to win the 1968 US Open Men's Championship, making him the first and only Black man to do so. Arthur went on to win three singles Grand Slam titles, but he also found his place as a true role model and a leader off the court. He was a tireless activist in the Civil Rights Movement and a humanitarian deeply involved in AIDS education and ending apartheid in South Africa.

It took nearly 20 years for the truth about what Johnnie did for his brother to come out. It wasn't until they were adults that Johnnie told Arthur the real reason he signed up for a second tour with the Marines. Johnnie's quiet sacrifice—for his brother and his country—was truly a gift. I hope you remember Johnnie Ashe the next time you walk by a tennis court, see a match, or play a game yourself. Arthur Ashe changed tennis forever, but it wouldn't have been possible without Johnnie's help, support, and enduring love.

## ABOUT THE AUTHOR

photo credit: Madeline Gray

**Judy Allen Dodson** is all about books—reading them as a librarian, preserving them as an archivist, and writing them as an author. Her book, *Escape from . . . Hurricane Katrina,* was a Junior Library Guild selection. Judy is also the winner of the Society of Children's Book Writers and Illustrators (SCBWI) On-the-Verge Emerging Voices Award, the recipient of multiple North Carolina Arts Council grants, a Highlights Foundation Diversity Fellow in Children's Literature, and the regional co-ambassador for The Authors Guild. Judy has a passion for celebrating diverse children's literature and teaching young readers about history. She lives in Raleigh, North Carolina, with her family. Visit her online at judyallendodson.com and follow her on Twitter @jadlibrarian.

## ABOUT THE ILLUSTRATOR

photo credit: David Wilkerson

**David Wilkerson** is a Black American illustrator who was born in Denver, Colorado, and is currently based in Maryland. He developed a love for illustration during his time at the Savannah College of Art and Design and began his career in the animation industry, where he worked as a character designer, prop designer, and background designer. David has spent the past twenty-plus years creating the most authentic version of himself and believes two main things to be true—there is healing in storytelling, and it is the job of creatives to contribute to that cause.

For my loving husband, Darren, and fearless children, Jordan and Dylan.
Thank you for your unconditional love. –JAD

To my loving parents. Thank you for always encouraging me to follow
my dreams. –David

Published by Capstone Editions, an imprint of Capstone.
1710 Roe Crest Drive, North Mankato, Minnesota 56003
capstonepub.com

Library of Congress Cataloging-in-Publication Data
Names: Dodson, Judy Allen, author. | Wilkerson, David, illustrator.
Title: The Ashe brothers : how Arthur and Johnnie changed tennis forever /by Judy Allen Dodson ; illustrated by David Wilkerson.
Description: North Mankato, Minnesota : Capstone Editions, 2023. | Audience: Ages 8–11 | Audience: Grades 4–6 | Summary: "In 1968, Arthur Ashe climbed his way to the top of the tennis world in a time filled with racial tension and segregation. But his success didn't happen without help. Arthur's close relationship with his younger brother, Johnnie, was key to Arthur becoming the first Black man to break the color barrier in men's tennis. A layered story full of love, teamwork, and unconditional support, *The Ashe Brothers* tells the little-known story behind Arthur's Grand Slam win."— Provided by publisher.
Identifiers: LCCN 2022013079 (print) | LCCN 2022013080 (ebook) | ISBN 9781684465361 (hardcover) | ISBN 9781684466238 (pdf) | ISBN 9781684466269 (kindle edition)
Subjects: LCSH: Ashe, Arthur—Juvenile literature. | Ashe, Johnnie—Juvenile literature. | Brothers—United States—Biography—Juvenile literature. | African Americans—Biography—Juvenile literature. | Tennis players—United States—Biography—Juvenile literature.
Classification: LCC GV994.A7 D64 2023 (print) | LCC GV994.A7 (ebook) | DDC 796.342092 [B]—dc23/eng/20220502
LC record available at https://lccn.loc.gov/2022013079
LC ebook record available at https://lccn.loc.gov/2022013080

Designed by Sarah Bennett and Jaime Willems

**Bibliography**
Ashe, Arthur and Alexander McNab. *Arthur Ashe On Tennis: Strokes, Strategy, Traditions, Players, Psychology, and Wisdom.* New York: Random House, 1995.
Ashe, Arthur and Arnold Rampersad. *Days of Grace: A Memoir.* New York: Random House, 1993.
Ashe, Arthur and Clifford George Gewecke Jr. *Advantage Ashe.* New York: Coward-McCann, 1967.
Hubbard, Crystal. *The Story of Tennis Champion Arthur Ashe.* New York: Lee & Low Books, 2018.
Robinson Jr., Louie. *Arthur Ashe Tennis Champion.* New York: Doubleday, 1967.
Wright, David K. *Arthur Ashe: Breaking the Color Barrier in Tennis.* Berkley Heights, NJ: Enslow Publishers, 1996.

**Acknowledgements**
Thank you to Dr. Pauletta Brown Bracy, Kelly Starling Lyons, Sherry Buckner Sallee, Carole Boston Weatherford, The Schomburg Center for Research in Black Culture, Richmond Public Library, and Wake County Public Libraries (Mollie Huston Lee Collection). And a special thanks my editor, Alison Deering, and my agent, Lara Perkins, for always believing in this book.